ADAM, SINNER OR SAINT?

ANOTHER LOOK AT THE FALL

DR A.T. BRADFORD

NASB Scripture quotations taken from the New American Standard Bible®, Copyright © 1960, 1962, 1963, 1968, 1971, 1972, 1973, 1975, 1977, 1995 by The Lockman Foundation. Used by permission.

Copyright © 2012 Dr A T Bradford.

All rights reserved. No parts of this publication may be reproduced, stored in a retrieval system, or transmitted in any form or by any means, without the prior written permission of the publisher.

Thanks are due, as always, to my wife Gloria

Published by Templehouse Publishing, London, England.

www.templehouse-publishing.com

ISBN 978-0-9564798-6-0

The author may be contacted via: info@templehouse-publishing.com

Contents

Adam - Sinner or Saint?

Introduction — p 4

Chapter 1
The God Who Hides the Knowledge of Himself — p 7

Chapter 2
Why search the Scriptures? — p 13

Chapter 3
The Background to the Fall — p 19

Chapter 4
The Historical Background to the Understanding of Adam as a 'Type of Christ' — p 23

Chapter 5 The Fall — p 34

Chapter 6
God Equipped Men with the Grace to Care for their Wives and Children — p 39

Conclusion — p 43

References — p 44

Adam - Sinner or Saint?

Introduction

Adam is widely known throughout Christian and Jewish tradition as having been the means through which the curses associated with the fall afflicted humanity.

But does he fully deserve all of his bad press?

Was he, as some commentators have said, aligned to evil, showing contempt for what God had given him? (Adam plainly showed contempt for what God had bestowed on him - Matthew Henry.) [i] If so, how can he rightly be considered 'a type of the One who was to come' - i.e. of Jesus? (Romans 5:14).

To understand the events of the fall, it is necessary to put aside the pre-conceived ideas and prejudices of millennia of human thought and consider the biblical account afresh from the other direction in time, i.e. from beforehand and not in a way that is retrospectively influenced by tradition and convention.

When the fateful day dawned in Eden, Adam was exactly as God had designed and intended him to be. There is no Scriptural basis for the idea that sin had already entered into him or that his heart had already been corrupted. On the contrary, he stood in perfect and undiluted relationship with his Creator. Immature, yes. Naive, yes. Evil, no.

Historically, commentators have tended to interpret Paul's comment to the church at Rome that Adam was a 'type', 'foreshadowing' or 'pattern' of Christ by referencing Adam's place as the first of the old humanity and Jesus' as the first of the new humanity. However Adam is contrasted with Jesus for exactly that reason by Paul in 1 Corinthians 15:45-47 (KJV): 'It is written, the first man Adam was made a living soul; the last Adam was made a quickening spirit. Howbeit that was not first which is spiritual, but that which is natural; and afterward that which is spiritual. The first man is of the earth, earthy: the second man is the Lord from heaven.'

Paul deliberately places Adam's nature (created from the dust of the earth - hence 'earthy') in stark contrast with Jesus' nature (begotten by God as part of His eternal being and not made). Therefore it is unlikely that in writing to the Romans Paul was describing Adam in his humanity as a 'foreshadowing' of Jesus' humanity. This is because, as shall be seen, biblical 'types' are, by definition, likenesses, not contrasts. In 1 Corinthians 15 Paul is clearly drawing a stark contrast between Adam's earthly nature and Jesus' heavenly nature.

The other difficulty faced in comparing Adam and Jesus is that Paul's comment about Adam being a 'type' of Christ is made immediately after Paul has been considering Adam's sin. Romans 5:12-14 - 'Therefore, just as through one man sin entered into the world, and death through sin, and so death spread to all men, because all sinned, for until the law sin was in the world, but sin is not imputed when there is no law. Nevertheless death reigned from Adam until Moses, even over those who had not sinned in the likeness of the offense of Adam, who is a type of Him who was to come.' The context for Paul's statement on Adam's likeness to Christ is therefore, on the face of it, a highly unlikely one - sin - something that has long been puzzled over.

How was Adam, in his act of sin, a type of Christ? Is it possible that somehow Adam was 'the good guy', and not 'the bad guy' after all?

This book will seek to provide a new, somewhat simple yet previously unstated, answer to that question.

Chapter 1

The God Who Hides the Knowledge of Himself

Most of us have, at some point in our lives, enjoyed playing a game of 'hide and seek'. If we are parents, we may have enjoyed hiding the things we intended our children to take pleasure in finding, especially if the things we were hiding were things we knew that they wanted or needed.

What then, would be our experience if we hid such things but our children were too distracted by other things, or simply could not be bothered to want to join in the fun of looking for them? Disappointment? Frustration?

How does our Father in Heaven feel when His children cannot be bothered to search for the knowledge of Him? Do we, as His children, simply expect to receive everything 'on a plate', with no effort required on our part to acquire them?

Proverbs 2:1-7a reads: 'My son, if you will receive my words, and treasure my commandments within you, make your ear attentive to wisdom, incline your heart to understanding. For if you cry for discernment, lift your voice for understanding. If you seek her as silver, and search for her as for hidden treasures; then you will discern the fear of the Lord, and discover the knowledge of God. For the Lord gives wisdom; from His mouth comes knowledge and understanding. He stores up sound wisdom for the upright.'

What God has said - His words to us - are to be 'received' and 'treasured'. We are to be 'attentive' to them, because they contain the necessary 'wisdom', 'understanding' and 'discernment' that is needed both for everyday life with Him and for the particular enjoyment of our relationship with Him. His words are likened to 'silver', and, in verse 4, to 'hidden treasure' to be 'searched for'. When we find them, we 'discover the knowledge of God': the One who 'gives wisdom', and from whom comes 'knowledge and understanding' which He has 'stored up for the upright' - those who have set their hearts on seeking and following Him.

Jesus drew from this passage from the Old Testament Book of Proverbs in His teaching in Matthew 13:44. 'The Kingdom of Heaven is like a treasure hidden in the field, which a man found and hid again; and from joy over it he goes and sells all that he has and buys that field.'

God's kingdom is likened by Jesus to 'treasure hidden in a field'. The Greek word used for 'treasure' here is *'thesaurus'* which, as well as meaning a 'treasure chest', also means 'a collection of words', in this case words from

God. From this is derived its modern use as a type of dictionary. In Jesus' day this 'treasure' was probably Torah Scrolls, which in the Judean society of the time were the most precious commodity they had, and of immense value.

This meaning is confirmed by Matthew in the next two verses, verses 45 and 46, which liken the Kingdom of Heaven to 'a pearl of great value'. 'A pearl' meant a particular word of wisdom, and is still used in this sense in the English language today. Jesus' warning about not 'casting pearls before swine' (Matthew 7:6) carries this same meaning. Jews valued (and still value) their God-given Torah-wisdom above everything else they had. They understood that its meaning was not always immediately obvious. That is why the man in verse 44 'hid it again' - because he had been searching and found something of immense value that was not self-evident and obvious to all and sundry, and for the time being he wanted to keep it that way.

As an illustration of 'hidden treasure' within God's word, how was it that the baptism in the Holy Spirit went for centuries of Christian history largely hidden in meaning and application from the Church at large? Clearly evident on the pages of Scripture was important revelation about God's Spirit and His close involvement with, and so the empowerment of, His people. Yet the understanding and experience of those verses was not commonly and widely understood until the early twentieth century. Why? At least in part, because God had decided to hide it until that time. Just as, in relation to the incarnation, 'When the time had fully come, God sent His Son, born of a woman, born under law, to redeem those under law' (Galatians 4:4-5 NIV). God has a right time for everything. In the same way, when the right time had come, God revealed in a 'new' and fresh manner the work of the third Person of the trinity, and the Church has not been the same since.

Another example of 'hidden' truth subsequently disclosed by God is the inclusion of the wider nations of the world within the salvation plan of God, which previously had been mainly manifest among the people of Israel. As Paul wrote to the church at Rome, 'The revelation of the mystery which has been kept secret for long ages past, but now is manifested, and by the Scriptures of the prophets, according to the commandment of the eternal God, has been made known to all the nations, leading to obedience of faith' (Romans 16:26). And to the Ephesians: 'You can understand my insight into the mystery of Christ, which in other generations was not made known to the sons of men, as it has now been revealed to His holy apostles and prophets in the Spirit; to be specific, that the Gentiles are fellow heirs and fellow members of the body, and fellow partakers of the promise in Christ Jesus through the gospel' (Ephesians 3:4-6).

Matthew's gospel affirms Jesus' ministry in this light. 'This was to fulfil what was spoken through the prophet

Isaiah: "Here is my servant whom I have chosen, the one I love, in whom I delight; I will put my Spirit on Him, and He will proclaim justice to the nations. He will not quarrel or cry out; no one will hear His voice in the streets. A bruised reed He will not break, and a smouldering wick He will not snuff out, till He leads justice to victory. In His name the nations will put their hope" (Matthew 12:17-21).

With the coming of the New Covenant, the Kingdom of God was made open by faith to all the nations. This was something 'new' that could in fact be seen in the Old Testament, but which was not commonly understood until after Jesus' death and resurrection.

A further example of 'hidden' truth in the word of God is Luke 2:42-52. Luke clearly and deliberately sets out the impact that the 12 year old Jesus made upon the doctors of the law who ran the rabbinic university of Bet Midrash at the Temple in Jerusalem. This is the only account of Jesus' childhood that the gospels provide, and Luke surely gave it for a good reason. As the Torah-prodigy son of devout Jewish parents, the now openly and scholastically recognised genius of the boy from Nazareth would have ensured His following the same academic pathway taken by Saul of Tarsus / the Apostle Paul, who later 'sat at the feet of Gamaliel' in formal Torah scholarship (Acts 22:3). Being on an altogether greater level than Saul/Paul, Jesus ministered truth in a unique way and certainly in a completely different way to the existing Jewish Torah scholars. Yet Jesus would certainly have gained parity with them because His vastly superior knowledge of Torah was now evident to them all. The giver of Moses' law, from Mount Sinai, was now busy expounding that same law to the most senior teachers of Moses' law. To obey that law the doctors, and also Mary and Joseph as devout Jews, would certainly have followed its injunction and hence their legal duty to enrol Jesus in formal rabbinic and Torah scholarship according to the level of His ability. [ii] To do anything less would have been contrary to the law and the custom of their society in relation to their greatest asset - Torah, including the oral Torah handed down from Moses. It would also have been completely contrary to human nature in a society that highly valued education in the law. Yet how is it that this simple conclusion was not put forward until 2010? [iii] Could it, too, have been hidden?

This book will put forward a new explanation for Paul's comment in Romans 5:14, showing exactly how Adam, even in his sin, was an exact 'type' or 'foreshadowing' of the One who would save mankind from the consequences of that same sin. Could God have hidden that too, for millennia, for a future time? And has that time now come?

Chapter 2

Why Search the Scriptures?

Jesus, speaking in John 5:39 to those who had yet to believe in Him, said 'Search the scriptures; for in them ye think ye have eternal life: and they are they which testify of me' (KJV).

The first reason why we need to 'search the Scriptures' is because God has commanded us to. The reason for this is that they contain many things helpful to our life and relationship with Him that are not immediately obvious to simply a casual perusal of His word. 'Searching' implies study, and involves the application of our minds in harmony with the illuminating power of the Holy Spirit.

A second reason why we need to search the Scriptures is that the New Testament which we have in English is two languages removed from that spoken by the majority of the New Testament authors. The majority certainly all thought and most wrote, in the Hebrew language. This was then put into Greek as the most widely understood language of the day in which to widely circulate important information. These Greek manuscripts are what form the basis for New Testament translation. In the case of the gospels, they are certainly not the very words spoken by Jesus, who conversed and taught in Aramaic and Hebrew (although he almost certainly would have known Greek). So an effort must be made to connect the written Greek with the original language of the speaker.

A third reason for searching is that apart from being two languages removed, the process of accurate translation is further complicated by one of the stages involving a jump of culture and people-group as well as language. The writers of the Greek texts were not themselves Greeks. They were putting their Jewish Hebraic, God-inspired thought into the language of a very different people group and culture. It is not the case that the Greek of the New Testament can be approached in exactly the same way as the Greek of, say, Aristotle or Plato, who were writing in their primary language and with fellow-Greeks as their primary audience. The Greek lexicons used by translators of the New Testament necessarily render the Greek usage and Greek meanings of the Greek words. They do not normally focus on the particular way that first century Jewish, Hebrew-speaking Judeans used those same Greek words. Therefore a potential difference exists similar in essence to the difference between a North American's use of English and the British use of English - broadly similar but with a few distinct and pertinent differences. For example, a holiday spent enjoying the Norfolk Broads could mean two very different things depending on whether that language was used by an Englishman (to whom 'broads' are a type of canal) or by a North American (to whom 'broads' mean young women!)

A fourth reason why we need to search the Scriptures is that much of what is taught nowadays in relation to the Bible tends to be theologian-centred rather than Bible-centred theology. In other words, the views of men and women in relation to the Bible are what are being concentrated on rather than the Bible itself. This simply serves to increase the separation between the Bible and the believer, with the focus being on what the man or woman believed rather than primarily on what the Scripture itself actually says. For example, much of the modern understanding of salvation and the atonement is based on the teachings of John Calvin and Jacobus Arminius rather than primarily focussing on the relevant Scriptures and their meaning in relation to the Hebrew minds of the authors and the audiences concerned.

A fifth reason why we need to search the Scripture is that in any form of translation, whether across cultural groups or not, there is generally always a choice of possible word available to the translators. This is well illustrated by the Amplified Bible, which provides a list of possible translations for each of the major Greek words used in the New Testament. The best choice of word in translating a text is inevitably determined by an understanding of the context, including history, culture and known behaviour of the people group concerned. Consequently some prior knowledge of the speaker or writer's cultural background is essential to accurate and meaningful translation. A writer who is a Pharisee and hence a scholar of the law will often use words in a different way to a comparatively lesser educated person.

An illustration of these translation issues is the rendering into English of the Greek word *'tekton'*, which was the profession of Joseph, Jesus' earthly father, and so by extension of Jesus Himself. This is hugely important in correctly placing Jesus in the Judean society of His day. Of the two best known Greek lexicons, Liddle and Scott's lexicon translates 'tekton' as 'carpenter', whereas Slater's lexicon renders 'tekton' as 'craftsman' or 'architect'.

Which is the best choice of translation? The answer is determined by the first century Judean Jewish use of the word 'tekton' rather than the myriad of different Greek uses. The Jewish uses are mainly found in the New Testament itself and in the contemporaneous writings of Josephus Flavius, a Jew who served as the official historian of Judea on behalf of the ruling Roman empire, and who also wrote in Greek.

From a New Testament perspective the Apostle Paul in 1 Corinthians 3:10 describes the 'tekton' as employed in 'laying a foundation', and is accordingly universally translated as 'builder', despite Matthew and Mark's use of 'tekton' always being rendered in the traditional way as 'carpenter'. Josephus describes the work of the 'tekton' in even more detail than Paul; namely as that work done by the thousand priests who were conscripted to construct the

Temple on behalf of Rome's client king, Herod the Great. The Temple sanctuary was 166 feet tall, and the Temple site had foundations with depths of up to 200 feet, with foundation stones weighing up to 400 tons; hence the aptness of Paul's description of 'laying a foundation'. Herod needed Jewish tektons for whom the elitist priests would have sufficient respect to be amenable to being trained by them. Joseph was a Judean devout Jewish tekton and is highly likely, in the relatively small population of the region, to have been one of the 10,000 'most skilled craftsmen' that Josephus documents [iv] as being employed locally by Herod, many of which would have been tektons.

In modern terms such as person as a tekton would employ skills found in the professions of architecture, structural engineering and construction, with structural engineer being the best single choice. 'Tekton' is the second part of the Greek compound word '*architekton*', meaning 'architect'. Hence a 'master tekton' was, in Greek, an architect. This provides a vastly better understanding in the context of Paul's use of the word in 1 Corinthians 3:10, because 'master-carpenters' do not lay foundations. The choice of 'carpenter' with which to translate the profession of Joseph and Jesus has significantly coloured in an incorrect manner our understanding of Jesus' humanity.

The alternative of 'architect' or 'structural engineer' much better matches Jesus' teaching illustrations (from which carpentry is conspicuous by its absence), the news of a tower in Siloam that had fallen down (Luke 13:4), His disciples' use of the Temple buildings (Mark 13:1) as a kind of distraction technique after a major dispute with the Pharisees, the absence of any practically-based objection to His claim to be able to re-build the Temple in three days (His hearers, taking him literally, only question His timeframe of three days), and Paul's (a tent maker) description of his ministry as being that of a master-builder or architect (1 Corinthians 3:10) as well as the many big building (and temple building) illustrations in Paul's (and Peter's) teaching compared to the complete absence of any tent-making illustrations in Paul's many writings.

What's in a word? In the case of 'tekton', quite a lot.

Chapter 3

The Background to the Fall

Adam was created in God's image and likeness out of simple single-chain molecules (dust), into which state the human body returns once its God-given life ('breath' - *'psuche'* - 'the soul') departs. Being the first of humankind to be made in God's image, Adam was given the role of the firstborn to fulfil in terms of responsibility for caring for his Heavenly Father's creation. Adam was created perfect, in God's image, but not yet fully mature. It was necessary for him to work, 'dressing / cultivating' (the Hebrew here is *'abad'* - 'to serve'), and to 'keep' the land. To 'keep' (Hebrew: *'shamar'*) carries the meaning of 'guarding' and 'keeping watch over'. [v] Adam tended the Garden of Eden, in order to grow in his role of taking responsibility. Because of his lack of completeness in maturity, though having been perfectly made in God's image, it was necessary for him to have a 'helper', Eve.

The word used here for 'helper' or 'help' in the Hebrew (Genesis 2:18) is *'ezer'*. Of the nineteen biblical uses outside the passage in Genesis chapter 2, all but four specifically mean 'help from God', and of the six examples found in the Pentateuch all are used in this way. Eve was therefore literally 'help from God', created by God especially for Adam's need at that moment. She stood in the place of God as much-needed 'help from God'.

Though God could have made Eve from dust, in exactly the same way that He had made Adam, He chose not to. Instead, in a final act of supreme creative genius, God made something considerably more complex both in terms of function and design than the male. [vi] God made Adam out of the 'dust of the earth' (Genesis 2:7), in other words from simple single-chain molecules. In the case of Eve, God took some of the most valuable thing that He had yet made - human flesh. Whether from Adam's 'rib' or from his 'side' (the Hebrew can be translated in either way), God took human DNA (deoxyribonucleic acid), which remains the most beautifully complex molecular structure known to man. A double helix in shape, its amino-acid protein configurations determine everything about human life, from longevity to the colour of the eyes. DNA was a fitting contrast to dust for God to use in expressing the closing of His creation, and one that well expresses the more complex nature of His design in imparting women's ability to support human existence both in-utero and in the early years of an infant's life and development, in a way that reflects God's own role in supporting life.

Just as a craftsman might eventually make a masterpiece and be able to stop manufacturing his craftwork, in order to teach others instead, so God has ceased His active work of creation following the closure of the sixth day in Genesis chapter 1, and now devotes Himself to teaching us His ways.

Adam was responsible not only for the Garden of Eden but now also for caring for his wife. He was to love and 'watch over' her, as well as care for the rest of the Garden.

Adam had received the commandment concerning abstaining from eating of the tree of the knowledge of good and evil prior to being joined in the Garden by Eve. While the Scripture does not record the content of what Adam passed onto Eve about God's command, he does not appear to have been very thorough, given Eve's response to the serpent - 'God has said, "You shall not eat from it or touch it, or you will die" (Genesis 3:3). Adam's duties of 'cultivating and keeping' the trees in the Garden had not excluded the tree of knowledge of good and evil. He would have had to 'touch' the tree to perform the tasks necessary to pruning and 'keeping'. The commandment simply prohibited the eating of its fruit (which, given the region concerned, is unlikely to have been an apple!)

God does not remove His children from the reach of temptation; rather, He places them amongst it and works in them to strengthen them and to help them resist it. The tree of the knowledge of good and evil had been deliberately placed by God in 'the middle of the Garden' (Genesis 2:9). 'In the midst' is, in Hebrew, *'tavek'*, meaning 'middle'.

God was not shielding Adam and Eve from temptation, rather, He was helping them face it in order to overcome it. In a similar way Jesus faced temptation from the devil (Luke 4:1-13) and overcame it.

Jesus did not pray (John 17:15) that His church 'might be taken out of the world', but rather that His Father would 'protect them from the evil one'. God does not always keep us away from temptation, but instead strengthens His children that they might, with His help, overcome it, and so grow and mature in their faith. Such was the case in the Garden of Eden.

Chapter 4

The Historical Background to the Understanding of Adam as a 'Type of Christ'

(Warning: This chapter contains scholarly quotations! Feel free to move to the next chapter and come back to this one.)

Romans 5:12-14 (NASB): 'Therefore, just as through one man sin entered into the world, and death through sin, and so death spread to all men because all sinned, for until the Law sin was in the world. But sin is not imputed when there is no law. Nevertheless, death reigned from Adam until Moses, even over those who had not sinned in the likeness of the offense of Adam, who is a type of Him who was to come.'

In this passage Paul uses the word 'type'. The Greek word used by him is *'tupos'*, which also means a 'likeness', 'example', 'figure of', 'pattern of' or 'print of'. [vii] 'Tupos' comes from *'tuptô'*, which means 'to strike'. The word was used for the process of impressing an image upon coins, whereby the coin's metal was heated and then struck powerfully with a hammer bearing an impression or mould, such that the image was then transferred onto the coin itself.

Vine's Expository Dictionary defines 'tupos' as meaning 'a blow' (from 'tuptô', 'to strike'), hence, '(a) an impression, the mark of a blow, (b) the 'impress' of a seal, the stamp made by a die, a figure, image, (c) a 'form' or mould, (d) the sense or substance of a letter, and (e) an ensample, or pattern in an ethical sense.'

'Typology' in Scripture represents a foreshadowing of a future person or event. We use a similar concept today in the related term, 'prototype', meaning the first one of a succession of items in the same category. Shadows are by nature the same in outline as the object creating the shadow. A 'type' is, by definition, something that is essentially the same as, or very similar to, the thing that it is foreshadowing. The emphasis is on similarity; a 'type' in Scripture is not a contrast, as the following examples clearly show.

Aside from Romans 5:14, the word 'tupos' is used in fourteen other verses in the New Testament. These are as follows:

1) John 20:24 - The 'print', or 'mark' of the nails in Jesus' hands, i.e. the holes left by the nails, necessarily being the same size and shape as the nails used to crucify Jesus.
2) Acts 7:43 - The worshipped 'images' of Molech (the god of the Ammonites) and Rephan (or Remphan, also known as Chiun), an Assyrian-Babylonian god based on the planet Saturn. These are both clearly images in the sense of

physical representations of two of the pagan idols worshipped by the Israelites at the time of their deportation to Babylon.

3) Acts 7:44 - The 'pattern' of the Tabernacle that Moses received on Mount Sinai, which formed the design template upon which the Temple was constructed, i.e. a plan of the design for the Tabernacle.

4) Acts 23:25 - The 'form' of the letter that Claudius Lysias, the commander of the Roman fort of Antonia adjoining the Temple in Jerusalem, wrote to accompany Paul to the Roman governor Felix in Caesarea. Luke reproduces the letter in its entirety, in the exact 'form' or 'manner' written by Claudius Lysias.

5) Romans 6:17 - The 'form' of teaching which the church at Rome committed itself to faithfully following. They were staying true to the exact teaching delivered to them by those who had come from Jerusalem with the gospel, and from Paul himself.

6) 1 Corinthians 10:6 - 'The examples' from the history of the people of Israel that Paul cites as having happened, in part, to provide valuable object-lessons to God's people who were to come after them. These 'examples' were: 'Our fathers were all under the cloud and all passed through the sea; and all were baptized into Moses in the cloud and in the sea; and all ate the same spiritual food; and all drank the same spiritual drink, for they were drinking from a spiritual rock which followed them; and the rock was Christ.' There are a number of 'types' mentioned here, notably a rock that provided water which

Paul cites as a 'type' of Christ, in addition to the passing through the Red Sea as a 'type' of Christian baptism.

7) 1 Corinthians 10:11 - The judgements that befell the rebellious Israelites are 'examples' to warn us against similar behaviour. God was quite willing to judge the same wrong behaviour in the church (e.g. Ananias and Sapphira whose deceptive behaviour is described in Acts 5:1-11). Paul warns that the same type of judgement may befall those who imitate such behaviour. Similar judgements were actually occurring in Corinth at the time of Paul's writing, as 1 Corinthians 11:29 makes clear in the context of the Lord's Supper.

8) Philippians 3:17 - Paul commands the church to note and copy those whose lives follow the 'pattern' of teaching that he delivered to them. These people are good examples because they are modelling the biblical way to live out their faith in the same way they had been taught by the Apostles.

9) 1 Thessalonians 1:7 - Paul commends the very good 'example' that the Thessalonians' faith and lifestyle are setting to the rest of the Macedonian and Achaian churches. This is because they had become 'imitators' of Paul and his apostolic team, and of the Lord Jesus Himself, and so represented the same faith practically being lived out in the way that Paul had taught them.

10) 2 Thessalonians 3:9 - Paul and his team's faith was offered as a 'model' to the Thessalonians; a good 'example' for them to follow in living out the same faith-based lifestyle.

11) 1 Timothy 4:12 - Timothy is exhorted by Paul to be a good 'example' to the other believers, one that they can copy.
12) Titus 2:7 - Titus too is urged by Paul to show himself as an 'example' or 'pattern' of good works, in order that others may have something visible to copy.
13) Hebrews 8:5 - As previously mentioned (in Acts 7:44), on Mount Sinai Moses was given a 'pattern' of the Tabernacle, i.e. construction drawings to follow in making the Tent of Meeting to the same dimensions as shown in the plans.
14) 1 Peter 5:3 - Peter exhorts the elders to whom he is writing to be good 'examples' to their flocks, again, that they might live out the same faith-based lifestyle.

To date, what have Christian scholars made of Paul's comment in Romans 5:14 regarding Adam as a 'type' of Christ?

The well respected commentary on the book of Romans by Douglas Moo gives the following interpretation:
'The word 'type' denotes those Old Testament persons, institutions or events that have a divinely intended function of prefiguring the eschatological age inaugurated by Christ - hence the word 'typology'. It is in this sense that Adam is a 'type' of Christ; the universal impact of his one act pre-figures the universal impact of Christ's act... Paul explains the typological relationship between Adam and Christ in verses 15-21. The similarity between the two

consists in the fact that an act of each is considered to have determinative significance for those who belong to each.' [viii]

For Moo it is the great significance of the two acts, Adam's sin and Christ's sacrifice, that provides the similarity between them necessary for them to be typological in nature. While both acts were undoubtedly of immense significance, the consequences are hugely dissimilar as is the perceived natures of the perpetrators. The significance of an act does not in itself provide a very complete basis for being a 'type'. Satan's rebellion and subsequent fall from Heaven was hugely significant in determining an outcome. Yet one would hardly describe the devil as a 'type' of Christ. Focussing on Adam's sin and its consequences, while being hugely significant, does not provide a well-rounded basis for a comparison to Jesus' act of mercy and sacrifice. But Moo is clear that it is similarity (and not contrast) that forms the basis for biblical typology.

Albert Barnes' 'Notes on the New Testament' commentary has the following to say about Romans chapter 5 verse 14: 'The expression 'He who was to come' is often used to denote the Messiah. As applied to Him, it means that there was in some respects a similarity between the results of the conduct of Adam and the effects of the work of Christ. It does not mean that Adam was constituted or appointed a type of Christ, which would convey no intelligible idea; but that a resemblance may be traced between the effects of Adam's conduct and the work of Christ. It does not mean that the person of Adam was typical of Christ; but that between the results of his conduct and the work of Christ there may be instituted a comparison, there may be traced some resemblance. What that is, is stated in the following verses. It is mainly by way of contrast that the comparison is instituted, and may be stated as consisting in the following points of resemblance or contrast.

(1) Contrast:

(a) By the crime of one, many are dead; by the work of the other, grace will much more abound (Romans 5:15).

(b) In regard to the acts of the two. In the case of Adam, one offence led to the train of woes; in the case of Christ, His work led to the remission of many offences (Romans 5:16).

(c) In regard to the effects. Death reigned by the one; but life much more over the other.

(2) Resemblance:

By the disobedience of one, many were made sinners; by the obedience of the other, many shall be made righteous (Romans 5:18-19). It is clear, therefore, that the comparison which is instituted is rather by way of antithesis, or contrast, than by direct resemblance. The main design is to show that greater benefits have resulted from the work of Christ, than evils from the fall of Adam. A comparison is also instituted between Adam and Christ in 1 Corinthians 15: 22 and 45. The reason is that Adam was the first of the race; he was the fountain, the head, the father; and the consequences of that first act could be seen everywhere. By a divine constitution the race was so connected with him, that it was made certain that, if he fell, all would come into the world with a nature depraved, and subject to calamity and death, and would be treated as if fallen, and his sin would thus spread crime, and woe, and death everywhere. The evil effects of the apostasy were everywhere seen; and the object of the apostle was to show that the plan of salvation was adapted to meet and more than countervail the evil effects of the fall. He argued on great and acknowledged facts - that Adam was the first sinner, and that from him, as a fountain, sin and death had flowed through the world. Since the consequences of that sin had been so disastrous and wide-spread, his design is to show that from the Messiah effects had flowed more beneficent than the former were ruinous.'

For Barnes, the typology being employed in Romans 5:14 is about contrasts. Even Barnes' section on 'resemblance' is actually contrast - as he says, 'antithesis, or contrast'. Barnes' focus misses the point that typology in the New

Testament, as shown in all the references above, is about likeness, and not about opposites or contrasts. Even the 'examples for warning' of 1 Corinthians 11 are likenesses, both in terms of historic events in the Israelite's history and in terms of the episodes of rebellious behaviour and judgement which were already evident in the fledgling church, be it in Acts 5 (Ananias and Sapphira's deceptive behaviour in the early church) or indeed the warnings in regard to participating in the communion meal given in 1 Corinthians chapter 11 verse 27. Wrong behaviour in the Old Testament was a foreshadowing of wrong behaviour in the New Testament, and Paul uses those illustrations from the Old Testament as warnings of a type of likeness of behaviour that is to be avoided. For Barnes, Adam as a 'type' of Christ (in the usual manner of foreshadowing) conveys 'no intelligible idea' - probably because Paul's context for his comment on typology in verse 14 is Adam's sin, which, on the face of it, is indeed very hard to align with Jesus' righteousness.

If Romans 5:14 follows the pattern of typology in the rest of the New Testament, then an answer to the question of how Adam's sin was, in some way, a likeness of Christ, will have to be sought in other areas than contrast. Lest we assume that Adam, in his sin, was a complete likeness of Christ, Paul does provide many contrasts in the following verses; however he introduces those contrasts in the first word of verse 15 with 'But', this being '*alla*', meaning 'nevertheless' or 'not withstanding'. [ix] This then brings in the opposites - how Adam was different to Christ. It does not reverse his earlier statement that Adam was a 'type' of Christ, or render that statement subject to a different use of the word 'type' than employed in the rest of the New Testament.

John Wesley's commentary on Romans sums up the issue of Adam being 'a figure of him that was to come' with 'Each of them being a public person, and a federal head of mankind.' For Wesley, the likeness between Adam and Christ is found in them being revealed as the one who ruled, in one sense or another, over mankind. This has been a common interpretation of the passage to date among scholars, and it is certainly true that Adam represents the old humanity and Christ, in His incarnation, represents the new. However the 'likeness' analogy necessarily stops there - there is no connection made or indeed any attempt to connect the actions of these 'federal heads'. Yet Paul's context in Romans 5:12-14 is in fact 'the sin of Adam', in other words it is an action-specific focus, and not merely a comparison of the two individuals' positions in relation to the rest of mankind.

Traditional Christian commentators from other church backgrounds have tended to share Barnes' view that Adam 'was a figure by contraries'. For example, 'By the first Adam, sin and death entered into the world; by Christ, justice and life.' [x] The problem is that these comparisons are based on the consequences of the respective actions, rather than on the action itself. Adam's sin led to death, Jesus' sacrifice led to life. Adam is associated with sin, Jesus is associated with righteousness. These are contrasts that cannot be brought together by the process of typology as laid down in the rest of the New Testament. To reconcile Paul's statement more fully, we must look elsewhere for the true meaning.

Chapter 5

The Fall

Genesis 3:3 makes it clear that Adam was present with Eve when the serpent began his dialogue with her. However Adam makes no attempt to intervene and bring any correction to the deceit. In 1 Timothy chapter 2 verse 14 (NASB), Eve is said to have 'fallen into transgression' ('the woman being deceived was in the transgression' - KJV). Eve's deception was something that Adam could have prevented. Perhaps Adam was curious to see what would happen if Eve did indeed eat of the tree's fruit. Being made in God's image and reflecting His likeness both Adam and Eve would have shone with the reflected glory of God, just as angels do (Luke 2:9).

When Eve ate of the fruit, God's glory would have ceased to radiate from her. A visible change in her would have occurred consequential to the act of disobedience.

To understand what followed we need to put ourselves in Adam's shoes. He was now faced with a choice. How did he feel when he realised that his failure to communicate properly to Eve all the Lord had said to him concerning the fruit had led to her losing the glory she had before God - the glory she shared with the angels?

How did Adam feel when he realised that he could and should have intervened, being present when the dialogue between Eve and the serpent was occurring and being in possession of first-hand knowledge of God's command concerning the tree?

How did Adam feel when he realised he had let both Eve and God down so badly? How did he feel towards the God who had given him the commission to care for Eve as 'his own flesh'? (Genesis 2:23).

How did Adam feel when he saw the priceless gift from God, whom he loved in a unique way over all God had made, and with whom he was now in a 'one flesh' relationship, suddenly lose the radiance of glory that marked both of them out from the animals that God had made and which inhabited the Garden with them?

How would Adam respond? Would he reject Eve, break their one flesh relationship, and ask God for another 'help from God'? Or would he realise that the only option for him in making amends both to her and to God would be for him to voluntarily join her in a state of loss of glory and in doing so throw himself on the mercies of his Father and Creator?

In a moment, Adam did what millions of men have instinctively done for their loved ones in the millennia that followed. Adam received the grace of God to lay down his life - his perfect relationship with his Father - for Eve, out of love for her, and a desire to fulfil his responsibility in caring for her as his Father had said to.

Adam's immediate and God-given desire was to sacrifice himself for Eve's sake. Even today men are willing to lay down their lives for their wives and loved ones. Why? Because it is in them, inherently, from God, and when the going gets tough, the tough get going. Millennia before Paul's command that husband's should lay down their lives for their wives, as Christ did for the church' (Ephesians 5:25), Adam did exactly that. Millennia before Paul was inspired by God to write 'Be imitators of God, as beloved children; and walk in love, just as Christ also loved you and gave Himself up for us' (Ephesians 5:1-2 NASB), Adam did exactly that for Eve, his wife. And that, simply that, is why Adam was a 'type of He who was to come' (Romans 5:14).

This act of self-sacrifice for the one Adam loved reflected exactly God's love, expressed in His Son, in lowering Himself into our sin-darkened world and laying down His life for the sake of His church, His bride (Revelation 21: 2 and 9).

Just as Adam chose to give-up his perfect relationship with his Father God, so Jesus laid aside His omniscience, omnipresence and omnipotence to become a man, God incarnate, but now fully dependent on His Father. Jesus voluntarily took on a lower state in terms of His dignity as the second Person of the trinity in a way that meant prayer, study, service and all the other aspects of His life that He modelled in His human form for us to imitate.

Adam too was forced to throw himself upon Father God's grace and provision for him in a place of weakness. As John wrote, 'We know love by this, that He laid down His life for us, and we ought to lay down our lives for the brethren' (1 John 3:16).

Jesus laid down His life in becoming an embryo in the womb of a virgin woman. He laid down His life in submitting Himself to two devout Jewish parents in their training and instruction in Torah, the very truths He Himself had delivered to Moses on Mount Sinai. He laid down His life in scholarship and work, as all religious and hence educated Jews did in first century Judea. He laid down His life in giving up the societal privileges associated with Temple-based Torah legal scholarship and instead journeying amongst the uneducated, ordinary men and women of the villages of Judea, bringing to them the truths that the other religious authorities of His day, who despised the uneducated masses, denied them.

Jesus laid down His life in daily hardships for which the foot-washing on the eve of His final Passover was but an example. He laid down His life in willingly submitting to the illegal trial and humiliation at the hands of the pagan

Romans and the Sanhedrin whose favour He had once known.

Jesus laid down His life in submitting to a trial before a dishonest Roman (Pilate) and ultimately, once and for all, in His death at Calvary. He laid down His life by descending yet further into Hades, the place of the dead, there to announce His victory over sin and death that His resurrection would be the final proof of for all time.

Jesus laid down His life for His bride, the church. And in exactly the same way Adam stepped down out of his uninterrupted relationship with his Father and into a world of sin hostile to himself, and ultimately under a curse, the curse that his disobedience to God in failing to protect Eve had cost. And he did so out of love for Eve, the one his Father had prepared for him as his bride. He did so in an act of self-sacrifice that he might fulfil God's purposes for him and so to ultimately be pleasing to his Father's call.

And in doing so Adam perfectly and exactly foreshadowed and typologically displayed the behaviour of 'the One who was to come' (Romans 5:14).

Chapter 6

God Equips Men with the Grace to Care for Their Wives and Children

One modern-day illustration of men's willingness to sacrifice for those they love may be found in the mundane area of sales of life insurance policies, which are taken out to benefit the survivors of a person's death.

Despite the large rises in the number of women working outside the home, most life insurance is still purchased by men. A recent study in the US showed that the majority of working women had no life insurance, and that most of those who did were under-insured. [xi] A recent study by UK insurers Bright Grey showed that more than half of working women had no life cover whatsoever and that 84% of working women did not hold income protection products which would pay them a regular income in the event of sickness or disability. [xii] Where both husband and wife work, the husband is the more likely to have taken out coverage to protect his wife than vice versa.

Self-preservation is an extremely strong human instinct. Yet history is littered with accounts of men who have instinctively and reflexly sacrificed their own lives for their wives or girlfriends.

A number of recent examples of this phenomenon occurred in Aurora, Colorado at a premier showing of 'The Dark Knight' (Batman) film, when a gunman killed twelve people and injured over seventy others. Of the twelve dead, four were men present who instinctively threw themselves over their girlfriends when the gunman opened fire with an automatic weapon in the darkness of the movie theatre.

Jon Blunk, aged 25, pushed his girlfriend Jansen Young to the ground and under the seats, throwing his body over hers, sparing her from injury. In so doing he took a bullet that ended his life. Simultaneously, 24 year old Alex Teeves was pushing his girlfriend Amanda Lindgren to the floor. "He pushed her to the floor to save her and he ended up getting a bullet", his aunt Barbara Slivinske later told reporters. [xiii] Likewise Matt McQuinn was at the same time using his own body to shield his girlfriend, Samantha Yowler. Witnesses later stated that 'he dove onto his girlfriend as the shooting started'. The fourth man to die in this way was U.S. Navy Petty Officer, 3rd Class, John Larimer. Larimer, aged 26, and his girlfriend Julia Vojtsek, aged 23, were sitting in the middle of the theater when the shooting began. "John immediately and instinctively covered me and brought me to the ground in order to protect me from any danger," Vojtsek wrote in a statement. "Moments later, John knowingly shielded me from a spray of gunshots. It was then I believe John was hit with a bullet that would have very possibly struck me. I feel very strongly that I was saved by John and his ultimate kindness." [xiv]

A similar story emerged from the wreck of the capsized Costa Concordia cruise ship that ran aground off the west coast of Italy at Giglio Island on January 14th, 2012. The widow of a Frenchman who died on the Costa Concordia luxury liner later told of how her husband sacrificed his life by giving her the only life jacket they had. "I owe my life to my husband," said Nicole Servel, aged 61, whose husband Francis was one of six people to die when the liner ran aground off the Italian coast. "He said to me 'Jump, jump'. And as I don't know how to swim, he gave me his life jacket. I was hesitant about jumping. So he went first. Then I jumped. I floated on my back," she told reporters. "I called to him, he shouted back: 'Don't worry! I'll be all right.' The water was barely eight degrees. And then, I never saw him again," said Servel, whose children had given her and her husband the Mediterranean cruise as a 60th birthday gift. [xv]

Another example of this kind of sacrifice occurred when a tornado hit Joplin, Missouri, USA, on May 22, 2011, killing one hundred and sixty one people. As their house was being ripped apart by the 200mph winds, Don Lansaw covered his wife's body with his own to save her from the flying debris. In doing so, he was punctured in the back and died saving her life.

Similar accounts also emerged from the Broad Arrow Cafe massacre in Port Arthur, a former penal colony in south-eastern Tasmania, Australia, on April 28th, 1996. Out of the thirty five people gunned down were Walter Bennett and Kevin and Raymond Sharp (both brothers), who all instinctively stood to shield their wives and were killed. Tony Kisten moved to shield his wife Sarah and was also hit. As he lay dying in his wife's arms, the Salvation Army member said: "I'm going to be with the Lord". Ex-RAAF officer Peter Croswell was lying on the floor, prostrate but protecting Thelma Walker and Pam Law. The three were initially unharmed but frozen in the hope the gunman would believe they were dead. Although the gunman fired at Crosswell, hitting him in the buttocks, the ex-RAAF officer did not move. It saved his life and theirs. 71-year-old retired horticulturalist Ron Jary and his friend Dennis Lever from Red Cliffs in Victoria's far north-west also both pushed their wives aside just moments before being shot. [xvi]

Why is that these wide variety of men reacted in this way towards those they loved? The fact that it happened instinctively, without the time necessary to consider what was happening, shows that it had been hard-wired into their natures by their Creator. It is by no means a completely universal trait, but one that was first displayed by their oldest ancestor, Adam of Eden.

Conclusion

Isn't it Obvious?

It is my conviction that Adam sacrificed himself for Eve, his bride; in just the same way that Christ sacrificed Himself for the church, His bride. In late 2012, this seems just as obvious to me as it did four years ago when God first taught it to me by the revelation of His Holy Spirit.

It is obvious, but it had been hidden. Fortunately God is still in the business, as the Head of the household, of bringing the new, as well as the old, out of the treasure that is His word (Matthew 13:52).

It is my hope that this understanding of Adam's sacrificial love for Eve will inspire husband's to follow Paul's instructions concerning their laying down their lives for their wives as Jesus did for us, His church. I also hope that this illustration will further increase our appreciation of Jesus' sacrifice and our gratitude towards Him, our All in all.

References

[i] Matthew Henry (1662 - 1714), Commentary on Romans
[ii] Mishna Avot 15
[iii] 'The Jesus Discovery - Another Look At Christ's Missing Years', published by Templehouse
[iv] Josephus Flavius, 'The Antiquities of the Jews', Book 15, Chapter 11
[v] Strong's Greek and Hebrew Dictionary
[vi] See 'The New Testament on Women, What Every Man Should Know', published by Templehouse
[vii] Strong's Greek and Hebrew Dictionary
[viii] Douglas Moo, 'Epistle to the Romans' published by W. B. Eerdmans
[ix] Strong's Greek and Hebrew Dictionary
[x] Haydock's Catholic Bible Commentary
[xi] www.wholesaleinsurance.net
[xii] www.theinsuranceservice.org
[xiii] NY Daily News.com
[xiv] Chicago Tribune, July 23, 2012
[xv] Reuters News Agency
[xvi] Victoria Examiner, May 1, 1996, and the Sydney Morning Herald, May 4, 1996.

www.ingramcontent.com/pod-product-compliance
Lightning Source LLC
Chambersburg PA
CBHW071846290426
44109CB00017B/1942